Spartan

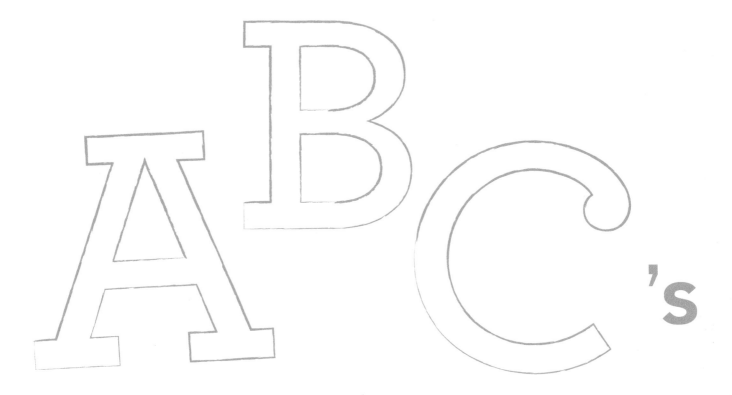

ABC's

By Courtney De Sena

Illustrated by Steven Mosier

Spartan ABC's
By Courtney De Sena
Illustration and Design by Steven Mosier

Published by Spartan Race, Inc.
Boston, MA 02110

ISBN: 978-0-9967749-0-1

Other available versions:
Digital Distribution
ISBN: 978-0-9967749-1-8

First Edition

For all the kids who don't have the necessities
For all the kids who don't have the luxuries
For all the kids who don't have the knowledge

This book is dedicated to you.

A

is for

Aroo! Aroo! Aroo!

B

is for

Burpee

down

jump & clap

C is for **Climbing**

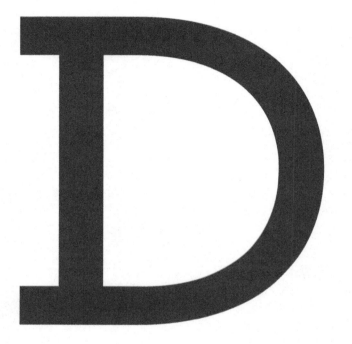

D

is for **Dirt**

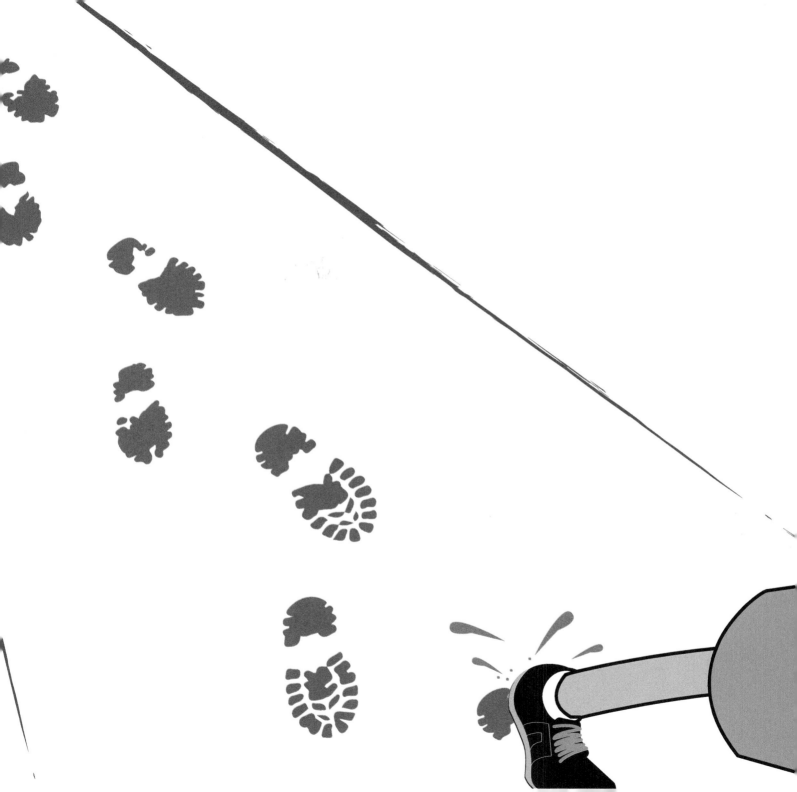

E is for **Energy**

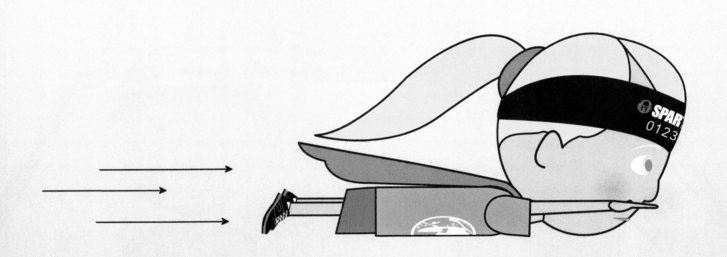

F is for Friends

is for

Green Juice

H

is for

Healthy

I is for

Incredible

J is for
Jump
Rope

K

is for **Kindness**

L

is for **Lifting**

M

is for **Muddy**

N

is for

Never
Give
Up

is for
Obstacle

P

is for
Playing

Q is for Quest

R is for Running

 is for Squat

is for **Tire Flips**

Up the Wall

U

is for

Up and
Under

Under the Net

V

is for

Veggies

W

is for

Winning

down

jump & clap

down

jum

X  is for
eXtra
Burpees

 clap

 down

 jump & clap

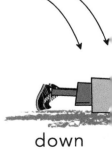 down

is for You

Z

is for

A Zillion Healthy Spartans Worldwide

Courtney De Sena grew up in Pembroke, MA, and went to Penn State on the first full soccer scholarship awarded to a woman. She helped lead the Nittany Lions to their first Big 10 title as a freshman and advanced to the NCAA Final Four as a senior. She currently oversees the De Sena Properties: Riverside Farm for weddings and events in Pittsfield, VT; Amee Farm, a small organic farm; and Amee Farm B&B. She is a mother, wife, marathoner, skier and coach of her son's soccer team. Courtney and Joe De Sena have four children.

Steven Mosier is a graphic designer based in New York City. Over the course of a 16-year career he has worked with major brands such as Ford, NASDAQ, the Museum of Modern Art, Socrates Sculpture Park, The Blanton Museum at the University of Texas, Phillips Auction house as well as real estate marketing and branding. His love for sports and fitness has found its way into his recent work with the Reebok Spartan Race, marketing and branding for private trainers, Crossfit gyms, and other fitness businesses. A near-death cycling accident in 2009 introduced him to obstacle racing, marathons, and Crossfit. He also enjoys playing and coaching ice hockey, snowboarding, softball, football and yoga.

Spartan NUMBERS

By Courtney De Sena

Illustrated by Steven Mosier

CPSIA information can be obtained
at www.ICGtesting.com
Printed in the USA
LVOW05s1102081215

465930LV00030B/606/P